Resilience:

A Choice for Everyday Living

**To the Point
Transformational Handbooks
for Business and Personal
Development**

 PUBLISHING

Dedicated to
Lydia

Contents

Building your resilience:

Understanding interactions with other people

Introduction
Resilience: A Choice for Everyday Living

For all of us there are occasions when life can sometimes be a real struggle. Day to day living can present numerous challenges requiring the maintenance of high levels of energy and performance. In addition, everyday life can demand inner steel and the courage to keep going through difficult times, as all of us will have periods when we are faced with the challenges that are part of the human condition such as disappointment, change, grief, illness etc.

Everyday resilience is about maintaining a sense of wellbeing and staying mentally strong, while effectively meeting the different demands presented to us and performing to our very best.

It may be that you spend the day biting your tongue whilst dealing with difficult customers or you work, or spend time with people who are unappreciative. It could be that you're having to carry on when riven with grief or in circumstances where you are putting on a brave face in order to reassure those around you.

Whatever the circumstances this handbook has been written to support individuals before reaching the point of personal distress, to help drive the negatives out of the way and provide support in maintaining purpose, motivation, values and focus. Resilience for Everyday provides a pathway from identification through to understanding and self-awareness and finally to recognising future action and beginning the start of a new journey.

The aim of Resilience. Resilience: A Choice for Everyday Living is to:

- Increase your knowledge and so create self-awareness
- Eliminate the effects of 'being present in body but not in mind and spirit'
- Mitigate stress symptoms
- Prevent the psychological and financial costs of reduced personal resilience for individuals, those around us, businesses, organisations and communities
- Reinforce or build up your everyday power and resilience
- Strengthen your confidence, enjoyment and participation in life.

About To the Point

'To the Point' are publications, which have been developed and written with different readers in mind, but in all cases designed for practical and easy use. Written in the form of bullet points, these quick to read handbooks encapsulate experience and knowledge drawn together throughout a career supporting the development of individuals and organisations.

The handbooks provide you with straightforward access to theories, ideas and frameworks proven to achieve results, account for behaviour and which can be integrated into everyday living.

'To the Point' is ideal for:

- Individuals who would like to increase their personal knowledge and understanding
- Organisations who wish to provide tool books for managers and teams
- People who want to learn quickly
- Discovering ideas, information and concepts to provide a springboard to deeper study

What do we mean when we talk about everyday resilience?

"Resilience is accepting your new reality, even if it's less good than the one you had before."

Elizabeth Edwards

Mental control

- Being mentally strong
- Mental energy and toughness
- Having personal control
- Inner strength
- Being composed
- Having the strength to do more than just cope

Mental Outlook

- Confidence, self-belief and efficacy
- An attitude of living life to the full, understanding that change can happen in an instant
- Remaining positive in difficult situations
- Energy (feeling alive, feeling wanted, feeling needed, feeling connected, feeling alert)
- Limiting the thinking that brings us down while increasing the thinking that lifts us up
- Being focussed
- Being persistent

- Being determined to see things through to the end
- Learning to act, rather than react

Self-maintenance

- Personal risk management. Strategies and plans to protect yourself for the present and the future
- Developing knowledge, skills and capabilities
- When necessary, having the courage to reach out and ask for help
- Building and nurturing relationships with other people

Recovery

- Withstanding stress and pressure
- Overcoming adverse events and experiences
- Bouncing back after a difficult/terrible event
- Recovering easily from hardship
- Planning and goal setting

Learning

- ◆ Coming through negative situations with more confidence, not less
- ◆ Having a growth mind-set
- ◆ Recovery and survival which results in learning and in turn leads to personal growth

"Life is not about waiting for the storm to pass. It's about learning to dance in the rain."

Unknown

Examples of circumstances that can lead to resilience being undermined

Relationships and Dealing with People

- Being in the company of people who are self-absorbed, withdrawn or have a defeatist attitude. People who:
    - ❖ Drain others rather than enliven
    - ❖ Do not have any passion
    - ❖ Are bored and boring
    - ❖ Are uncaring
    - ❖ Constantly act like the victim
- Being in the company of people who create an impression of confidence or apparent power by being outspoken, abrupt or loud. People who:
    - ❖ Seem charming and enthusiastic but who don't listen or who lack intimacy
    - ❖ Are always performing
    - ❖ Engage superficially
    - ❖ Are insensitive and/or overbearing and/or arrogant
- Being in the company of people who:
    - ❖ Are pessimist or who constantly worry
    - ❖ Like hearing bad news

- ❖ See disaster around every corner
- ❖ Who feel something awful is always going to happen
- ❖ Forecast catastrophe in every situation
- ❖ Have an urge to share their anxiety and apprehension
- ◆ Lack of supportive relationships
- ◆ Dealing with obstructive individuals
- ◆ Dealing with intransigent people who are locked into ways of doing things
- ◆ Dealing with bureaucracy
- ◆ Dealing with difficult personalities (In situations where we already know the person, it may lead to finding ourselves rehearsing how to tolerate them, this in turn can lead to a cycle of thoughts, feelings and behaviours)
- ◆ Failed interactions with people (e.g. with work colleagues, managers, neighbours, family, former friends etc.)
- ◆ Being trapped in an unhappy marriage/relationship
- ◆ Caring responsibilities

Disappointment/Expectations not met

- ♦ Job applications, interviews and other requests ignored or declined
- ♦ Joining an organisation full of enthusiasm and excitement to find that:
  - ❖ It is not as thought it would be
  - ❖ It is not supportive or positive
  - ❖ You become exposed to risks and threats
  - ❖ You are unable to make the changes or implement thing as had hoped perhaps due to rules and regulations or factors such as resistance or organisational inertia
- ♦ Separation and divorce
- ♦ Infertility
- ♦ Unrequited Love
- ♦ Failure to achieve goals

The events that we experience during our life

- ♦ Accidents leading to incapacity
- ♦ Illness
- ♦ Physical or psychological injury or trauma
- ♦ Loss, Bereavement, Grief

- Challenges to family, friends, colleagues, team-mates
- Loss of job and income
- Lack of money
- Debt
- Loss of identity due to job changes
- Feeling ground down in a despised job or career
- Aging

Our thoughts, feelings, attitudes:

- How we interpret events
- Thoughts of revenge
- Lack of purpose and meaning to life
- The attitude we form/position we take (decisions formed out of thoughts and feelings)
- Fear of the future
- Fear of change
- Fear of failure
- Fear of 'being found out', the sense of being an imposter – despite having qualifications etc. a belief that you are not good enough or shouldn't really be in a

particular role/mixing with a particular circle or group of people

Lack of/loss of personal control

- The workplace:
  - ❖ High levels of uncertainty (e.g. organisational restructure / redundancies / mergers
  - ❖ Role overload or juggling other responsibilities
  - ❖ Organisational changes which may be:
    Political
    Economic (more for less)
    Social (the rise of new trends, groups, thinking)
    Technological (work transformations, leading to a feeling of being left behind)
- Failure
- Expectations and demands placed upon us
- Lack of knowledge, skill or understanding
- Addictions

The context and surroundings in which we experience life and events:

- ◆ Culture. It is harder to maintain resilience/control if we are experiencing:
  - ❖ Negativity
  - ❖ Lack of cooperation
  - ❖ Isolation
  - ❖ Bullying
  - ❖ Tall Poppy Syndrome – Standing out so being knocked down
  - ❖ An organisation that doesn't want a dynamic force within it ('*We'll do as we've always done*' etc.)
  - ❖ A nasty, competitive culture
  - ❖ Inhibiting rules/regulations/procedures
- ◆ The ambience or atmosphere and appearance of the environment.

The effects upon us when resilience is reduced

"*Obstacles, of course are developmentally necessary: they teach kids strategy, patience, critical thinking, resilience and resourcefulness.*"

Naomi Wolf

Under pressure

- Difficulty relaxing or 'turning-off'
- Dissatisfied
- Resentment
- Rigid ideas
- Distorted ideas
- Irritation
- Over-reacting
- Unable to cope
- Anger

Deflated

- Low mood
- Lack of interest
- Lack of energy
- Passion for life dwindles
- Loss of appetite
- Sense of defeat
- Weary
- Worn out

Weakened

- Denial – 'keep soldiering on'
- Poor decision making
- Poor productivity/output
- Accident prone
- Negative self-critical thoughts
- Sense of having let people down
- Guilt
- Shame
- Confidence dented
- Self-esteem diminished
- Personal core values shaken or eroded
- Reduced participation and contribution
- Visibility lowered
- Absence
- Social avoidance/withdrawal
- Loneliness
- Fatalism

Lowered resilience may lead to stress

"*That which does not kill me, makes me stronger.*"

Nietzsche

Different types of stress

- **Overstress**
  - ❖ This is when we take on more than we can handle. We may become workaholics or push ourselves too hard with deadlines. We experience too much stress.

- **Distress**
  - ❖ This is bad stress. It is persistent stress when excessive demands are placed upon us and we perceive that we cannot cope or we actually cannot cope, adapt and resolve the situation. If it is relentless and severe it can lead to ill health.

- **Under stress**
  - ❖ This is when there is too little stress; we experience a lack of stimulation or boredom.
  - ❖ Apathy and ennui ('Seen it all before')
  - ❖ Feeling a sense of emptiness and questioning the meaning of life

♦ **Eustress**

    ❖ This is the stress we experience when we are facing enjoyable challenges. Eustress can provide a sense of meaning, hope, vigour and satisfaction. However, if a challenge is too great a tipping point can be reached leading to overstress. For example:

            Watching scary films

            Competing in sports

            Doing exciting things like going on a rollercoaster ride

Stress Responses

"He who has a why to live for can bear almost any how."

Nietzsche

Acute Stress

Recent, anticipated or intense demands and pressures may lead to problems:

- ◆ Muscle Problems
    - ❖ Tension headaches
    - ❖ Back pain
    - ❖ Pulled muscles and tendons
    - ❖ Jaw pain

- ◆ Stomach, Gut & Bowel Problems
    - ❖ Heartburn
    - ❖ Acid stomach
    - ❖ Flatulence
    - ❖ Diarrhoea
    - ❖ Constipation

- ◆ Circulation & Nervous System
    - ❖ Elevated blood pressure
    - ❖ Rapid heart beat
    - ❖ Heart palpitations
    - ❖ Dizziness
    - ❖ Sweaty palms

- ❖ Cold hands and feet
- ❖ Shortness of breath
- ❖ Chest pain

- ♦ Mood
  - ❖ Short-tempered
  - ❖ Irritability
  - ❖ Always in a hurry
  - ❖ Hostile
  - ❖ Abrupt
  - ❖ Ceaseless worry

Chronic Stress

This is the persistent stress that individuals get used to. Mental resources have been depleted through long term attrition. May lead to:

- ♦ Violence
- ♦ Heart Attack
- ♦ Stroke
- ♦ Suicide

Self-Awareness Check

Stress Responses

"Success is not final; failure is not fatal: it is the courage to continue that counts."

Winston Churchill

Sometimes we get stuck in a way of thinking, feeling or behaving, all of which have consequences. For any decision or course of action that we choose to take there is a *'price to pay'* Here are just a few different examples:

Being highly ambitious

- Positives might be that you:
  - Enjoy financial wealth
  - Have the admiration of others
  - Lead an enviable lifestyle
- Negatives might be that you:
  - Become selfish and anti-social
  - Are weighed down with responsibility, demands and anxiety
  - Have an overwhelming fear of failure & of losing face

Staying in an unsuitable relationship

- Positives might be that you:

- ❖ Fit in and conform to judgements made by family, friends, neighbours, the community
- ❖ Live in a jointly funded property that you might not otherwise be able to afford
- ◆ Negatives might be that you:
  - ❖ Feel isolated, lonely, depressed
  - ❖ Are subject to unacceptable treatment

Unhappy in your job

- ◆ Positives might be that you:
  - ❖ Are getting a wage and *'It's not all bad' 'There's always the weekend'*
  - ❖ Are meeting the expectations of others
- ◆ Negatives might be that you:
  - ❖ Find difficulty sleeping and go into work with a sense of dread
  - ❖ Are deeply unhappy and demotivated
  - ❖ Experience 'burnout'

Think about the situations that cause you to feel the symptoms of stress.

- Remind yourself that all your choices and decisions mean that one thing is being forfeit for another.
- How would you like things to be?
- Have you reached a point where you think it isn't worth trying anymore?
- Are the negatives outweighing the positives?
- Are you avoiding action because it is easier to keep the status quo and have the approval of other people?
- Are you worried about the negative reactions of others?
- What do you need to do to alleviate the stress?
- What appropriate action can you take?
- What goals need to be made and achieved?

There are many forms of resilience…

Steven Spielberg

Photograph: Courtesy Yuri Turkov / Shutterstock.com

Reportedly rejected by both the University of Southern California and UCLA, at least once each, the man who has given us "Shindler's List," "Jaws," "E.T." and "Jurassic Park" could not get into the school of his choice and instead chose to go to college, he then dropped out, after he was offered a movie deal. However, he returned in 2001 and graduated with a BA in 2002. When asked why, Spielberg told the Telegraph that his younger children made him realise the importance of completing his education. "They began saying, 'Why do we have to go to college? Dad didn't graduate and he's really successful,' " he says. "I thought I'd better get that degree and get it fast, so I did."

Source: Telegraph
Spielberg: Why I went back to college

Examples of Resilience

Mental Outlook In this example, Steven Spielberg is showing that he is open to variety and new experience so increasing the potential for new opportunities. In turn, new opportunities can widen your sphere and remind us of the abundance of life.

Self-Maintenance Returning to finish his degree Steven Spielberg showed that he was able to see things through. He also demonstrated how he valued his children and relationships with his family in that he wanted to help his children by showing the way and sharing experience.

Building your Resilience

Mental Control &
Mental Outlook

Cognitive Processes
How we think
Thought Processing

"It's fine to celebrate success but it is more important to heed the lessons of failure."

Bill Gates

How we think – thought processing

Understanding how we think and the processes that take place mean we are in a position to actively deliberate and take a measured approach to the situations that arise in our everyday lives and so adding to our powers of resilience.

Reacting and Responding to Situations

- Reacting or choosing to respond to circumstances, is an interplay between thoughts, feelings / emotions and our attitude / approach / physiology.

- When our emotions are running high it is 'hard to think straight'. If you are angry or crying, you can barely think at all. When emotions take over this is when hasty decisions take place, rash purchases are made, ill thought through risks are taken.

- When our physiology is altered our thinking can be altered too. For example, if you feel hungry it can be hard to concentrate. If you simply stub your toe you are momentarily distracted. If you feel unwell your thoughts may be influenced accordingly

A useful framework for understanding thought processing is recognising two types of thinking namely; Automatic and Controlled Thoughts

Automatic Thoughts. This is when thinking is:

- Like being on auto-pilot
- Effortless
- Intuitive
- In fast mode
- Instantaneously 'anchored' to previous knowledge, thoughts and assumptions

Concentrated/Controlled/Attentional Thoughts. This is when thinking is:

- Something that you are conscious of
- Concentrated
- Slow and deliberate

♦   A logical, intellectual response

When behaving or interacting it might be worth checking yourself and considering if your position is based upon automatic thoughts. Do you need time out to take a considered approach?

Thought Processing – The Process of Incubation

There are times when our minds are overwhelmed and we cannot come up with the answers to our problems. In these situations, be minded of the wisdom contained in the adage to *'sleep on it'*. Generally, the mind is always working including processing memories and solving problems. Sometimes we need to give it time to come up with answers; we need to allow the mind time to go through the process called incubation and gradually reveal information and solutions.

Self-Awareness Check

Thought Processing

Consider what comes first, the thought, the feeling or the approach? Try to recognise what is happening. Do you need to raise your level of consciousness? Are emotions clouding rational thoughts? Is a desire to take a rational approach leading you to ignore your 'gut' feeling?

♦ **Feelings & Emotions.**

For example, when beliefs are irrational, when we are lonely, disappointed, upset or angry etc.:

❖ We can barely think at all.
❖ We have less focus and concentration
❖ We cannot separate facts and information from imagination
❖ We can 'dig in' and defend our position
❖ Our feelings and emotions can perpetuate and make things worse – try to take a reality check

"*To know others is smart. To know yourself is wise.*"

Unknown

Building your Resilience

Mental Control & Mental Outlook

Cognitive Processes
How we think
Creating Frameworks

Cognitive Processes

♦ During our lifetime our minds build an organising structure for knowledge and of how things should be. This is called a Schema.

♦ During our lifetime our minds build up information about the roles we play and that others play. Our minds create messages about stereotypical events and who we are within the context of such events. These thought processes are called Scripts.

♦ Stored Scripts operate when for example:
  ❖ You perhaps walk into a room and a person you have never met before reminds you of someone else.
  ❖ Travelling on a journey, one place reminds you of another.
  ❖ The experience that you are going through now reminds you of an experience you had once before.

- ❖ The circumstance of your current situation reminds you of something in the past and your expectation is that things will be the same as before.

- ◆ The combination of Schemata and Scripts lead to the creation of a general set of ideas called Frameworks.

- ◆ Schemata and Scripts can be altered and influenced because we attempt to anticipate outcomes, create patterns, assume we know answers and fill gaps in our thinking – this is why Jokes, Illusionists, Magic Tricks and Ghost Stories are so effective.

- ◆ The outcomes, assumptions and patterns we create can sometimes be wrong. Our interpretation of events, the behaviour and intentions of others may not be correct which can lead to misunderstanding, doubt, mistrust, apprehension, cynicism and conflict.

Cognitive Dissonance

♦ Cognitive Dissonance occurs when we have to behave in ways that are at odds with the Frameworks we have created for ourselves, with our sense of control, thoughts, attitudes, beliefs and ideas. Typically, this might occur in the workplace where we have to behave in a way at odds with our feelings. For example, being required to be polite with customers who are being rude or aggressive. We either:
  ❖ Dig in and defend
  ❖ Collude and comply and justify our decisions to ourselves
♦ Over the long term both options lead to lowered resilience.

"If you look back all the time, you will trip up going forward."

Unknown

Self-Awareness Check

Creating Frameworks

"*Courage is resistance to fear – mastery of fear, not absence of fear.*"

Mark Twain

Scripts, Schemata and Frameworks

♦ The person you were years back is different to the person you are now. You have had more experience, you understand more and you are wiser. What worked or was expected of you when you were aged five may not apply at the age of 45!

♦ What life was like for you 20 years ago is different from how life is now. Change has happened around you.

♦ You cannot change the past but you can change your present. A focus on the past can obscure your own ability and power to change your thinking.

♦ Are the scripts, schemata and frameworks that you have created useful in your world today? Do they really still apply? Are they holding you back?

Cognitive Dissonance

- Are you having to behave in a way which is inconsistent with your beliefs and values?
- Are you downplaying your own feelings or decisions or wants and needs?
- Are you justifying negative experiences in order to cope with them?
- Are you maintaining commitments which are not right for you in order to avoid losing face?
- Why are you letting a particular situation persist?
- How can you change the situation?
- Do you need to change yourself or your own way of thinking?

Building your Resilience

Mental Control &
Mental Outlook

Cognitive Processes
How we think
Reasoning

Cognition – Anchoring Effect

- ◆ The anchoring effect is related to our automatic thoughts. It means that because of previous experiences and events etc. we create associations. For example:
  - ❖ We reason that because X happened when Y was present that the same will happen every time in the future. This explains why athletes and people engaged in sport have 'lucky' socks or other articles of clothing that they keep wearing because they believe it helped them when they had some success. Many people keep Lucky Charms and talismans for the same reason.

The problem with the anchoring effect is that:

- ◆ It can lead to a dependency upon associations which can become problematic:
  - ❖ For some people, high levels of anxiety are created if they cannot perform particular rituals. For

example, this might be an individual who is unable to leave the house without performing and going through a set routine.

- ❖ It may mean that in an instant we make a decision about someone because they look like someone else and we develop cognitive bias.
- ❖ It can trigger emotions, behaviour and sensations which lead to negative self-talk and self-sabotage

Cognition – Reframing

- ◆ Erving Goffman stated:
    - ❖ *'Our capacity to reframe a situation can powerfully transform our experience of it'*
- ◆ It has been identified that we can reframe even the most positive messages so that they fit with our own negative self-image: For example: the message is being delivered by someone who:
    - ❖ *'Is just being kind'*
    - ❖ *'Has poor judgement'*
    - ❖ *'Who wants something in return'*
    - ❖ *'Is untrustworthy'*

Cognition - Self-Sabotage

Faulty scripts, schemata and reframing mean that we may have a tendency to think in such a way as to depress our positive mental outlook and distort our powers of reasoning. For example:

- Discounting the positive
  - ❖ *'If I can do it, it doesn't count'*

- Rationalising
  - ❖ *'It's not really a problem'*
  - ❖ *'It's only a small problem'*
  - ❖ *'It's not worth worrying about really'*

- Sense of Entitlement
  - ❖ *'I expect all people to treat me with kindness & consideration'*
  - ❖ *'I should easily be able to get what I want'*

- All or nothing thinking
  - ❖ *'You win or you lose'*
  - ❖ *'It's right or it is wrong'*
  - ❖ *'I'll do it now or not at all'*
  - ❖ *'I won't have time'*

- ❖ *'It's too hard/difficult'*
- ❖ *'It won't work'*
- ❖ *'Tried it before'*
- ❖ *'I'll probably never get around to it'*

- ◆ Mind reading
  - ❖ *'S/he didn't look at me therefore I have done something wrong'*

- ◆ Approval
  - ❖ *'I must do well to win the approval of other people'*

- ◆ Fortune telling
  - ❖ *'I just know it will be awful'*
  - ❖ *'It's not going to happen – I never get what I want, I only ever get what I don't want'*

- ◆ Catastrophizing
  - ❖ *'OMG this is SO terrible'*
  - ❖ *'If that happens, this will happen etc.'*
  - ❖ *'Everything is awful'*

- Personalisation
  - ❖ *'It's all my fault'*
  - ❖ *'I'm the one to blame'*
  - ❖ *'I can't change'*
  - ❖ *'It's not me'*
  - ❖ *'I'm stupid'*
  - ❖ *'I can't see myself doing it'*
  - ❖ *'I've always been like this'*

- Generalisation
  - ❖ *'I never get what I want'*
  - ❖ *'It's always the same'*

- Labelling
  - ❖ *'I did something bad, therefore I am bad'*
  - ❖ *'I said something foolish, therefore I am foolish'*

- The reasons for self-sabotaging may be:
  - ❖ Internalised messages received from any number of sources and at any time of life. For example:

> Critical or neglectful parents/carers
> Unsupportive or destructive partners
> Bullies (in any environment)
> Oppressive workplace colleagues

❖ Low mood or even depression

❖ Due to distorted thinking as there has been no one standing behind you and providing alternative or positive feedback

❖ Due to thoughts and emotions being negated by others

Cognition – Creating our world

We have the capacity to create different worlds for ourselves:

♦ The real world – based on facts and actuality

♦ An imaginary world – this is the world where we plan for things that may never happen, this is the world where we can self-sabotage.

♦ A world where we reinforce either the negatives or the positives

♦ A world where we anchor events and experiences to previous incidents

Self-talk

♦ If you have ever received encouragement from someone else recall your memories of being given support and how it felt, remember their words such as:

> *'You can do it'*
> *'You are going to be brilliant'*

♦ When you need to give yourself some positive self-talk, instead of speaking in the first person and saying things like *'I will do it'* say *'You can do it'* as if you are hearing the words are being said by someone else. Otherwise if you are feeling a bit low or lacking in self-belief you won't believe what you are saying!

♦ Think about the advice that you would give to someone else if you were trying to help them feel upbeat or to make a positive decision. Give the same advice to yourself, give yourself some positive self-talk:

> *'Keep calm'*
> *'Stay strong'*
> *'Everything will be all right'*

- Stop your negative thinking by distracting yourself. When you become aware that you are self-sabotaging try to switch your thinking on to something else by changing what you are doing or by purposely changing your thoughts
- Use reframing to give yourself some positive self-talk. For example, you have been asked to deliver a difficult presentation at work:

> Self-sabotaging
> > *'I'll probably clam up.'*
> Re-framed
> > *'I've never been lost for words before; I know that by being prepared I have been successful in the past'*

Self-Awareness Check

Reasoning

- Consider, are you engaging in self-sabotage, do you need to give yourself some positive self-talk or to re-frame your thoughts?

- Engage in some critical thinking: Are you caught in a habit that is blocking you and maintaining a cycle of effects and consequences?

- Be aware of your inner voice. When it says something negative, employ a stop mechanism to alter your thinking: Take a few moments and do some concentrated deep breathing or if there is little time, intervene with some positive self-talk.

- You are not psychic. You do not know what other people are really thinking and feeling.

- 80% of people that you meet in your lifetime are likely to have no deep feelings about you. Most of the time, most of the people are not thinking about you or judging you and so ignore what you think others are thinking of you and do your own thing.

♦ Practice in your head doing things right. See yourself, hear yourself, feel yourself winning, not losing.

♦ Imagine doing things differently. Think how it will be when you have made the change:
   ❖ What will you say to yourself?
   ❖ How will you feel?
   ❖ How will you look?

Building your Resilience

Mental Control & Mental Outlook

Cognitive Processes
How we think
Decision Making
Planning &
Locus of Control

There are many forms of resilience…

Albert Einstein

Photograph: Courtesy Bangkokhappiness/ Shutterstock.com

As we all know Albert Einstein was considered a genius by the time he was in his twenties, however he didn't start off showing his brilliance, in fact he hated formal education and rebelled against school. Many teachers stated in their reports that he "would never amount to anything".

Source: BBC iWonder
Albert Einstein: A life spent re-imagining physics

The text shown above is very interesting from the point of being resilient for as we know Einstein went on to become one of the world's leading intellects and influences of his age. As a consequence, his works and intellectualism were targeted by the Nazis who included him in a list of enemies with a bounty on his head. He was forced to leave Germany and although he was without a permanent home he actively worked to get other scientists out of Germany through his connections all over the world with politicians, celebrities, royalty and others. His letter to Roosevelt about concerns over nuclear technology is considered a pivotal document of World War Two.

Examples of Resilience

Mental Outlook

Throughout his life Einstein displayed boundless energy and from a very young age he had a curious mind (which was at odds with the formalities and studies imposed by his school).

Mental Control

Einstein was not bowed by the dangers and threats he faced during the 1930's and 1940's instead he displayed an inner strength. His strength of character had a profound effect not only in terms of his own level of resilience but on the lives of others.

Self-Maintenance

Despite his prolific output in terms of the physical world, Einstein invested time in his own relaxation (he was a sailor and musician). In addition, Einstein had created relationships across the world which, meant that he had considerable support in fulfilling his potential.

Recovery

Einstein overcame numerous life experiences, including seeing the struggle of his parents, the failure of his own marriages, his move from his homeland and the development of the nuclear bomb being at odds with deep and long held values.

Learning

Einstein came through his life experience as a campaigner for equalities and against war.

Locus of Control

Our sense of control is usually situated on or between the boundaries of two positions. This concept is described as our Locus of Control. An Internal Locus of Control refers to the belief that an individual can have full control over their life and that they count when it comes to having an effect upon the world around them. Alternatively, some people see life as lots of forces over which they have little control, with fate and luck playing a big part in outcomes, in other words they have an External Locus of Control.

External Locus of Control

Typical characteristics and behaviours of people who see decision making and planning outside of their control:

   ♦   It's always the fault of somebody else

- Little confidence in personal ability to shape own destiny
  - ❖ *'It's in the lap of the Gods'*
  - ❖ *'It's being in the right place at the right time...'*
  - ❖ *'It's not what you know, it's who you know'*
- Fate and chance determine the end results
- The direction of local, country and world affairs is out of their hands
- Absolve responsibility
- Fear responsibility
- Assume that people will judge them harshly no matter what they do
- Moan, but don't do anything about the situation:
  - ❖ *'If only I had...'*
  - ❖ *'It's entirely your fault...'*
  - ❖ *'If it wasn't for you I could have been/done...'*
- Blind adherence to:
  - ❖ Religious doctrine or other beliefs
  - ❖ Socially prescribed fashion, cultural mores
  - ❖ The dictates of people around them such as an organisation

- External drivers such as:
  - ❖ The projections of previous generations
  - ❖ The messages and approval of parents as received when a child
  - ❖ Conformity to a social division

Internal Locus of Control

Typical characteristics and behaviours of people who believe that they have complete control when making decisions and planning. They:

- Create opportunities, not by being pushy but by being smart, value driven and realistic
- Believe hard work brings results
- Influence the environment through their own actions
- Recognise that they can change their behaviour and influence the behaviour of others
- Look to influence people's appraisal of them
- Accept and adapt to events to meet personal needs

- ◆ Consider it is important to get involved and participate if change is to be achieved at any level
- ◆ May be perfectionists

Locus of Control

There are some occasions when it may be wise to take responsibility and make decisions to take control. For example:

- ❖ Planning the events of life. These might include being interviewed for a job, preparing for exams, taking a driving test, arranging a wedding or booking a holiday.
- ❖ To help life run smoothly. For instance, booking a service for the vehicle that you ride/drive. Having a kitchen cupboard stocked with basic foods. Backing up computer files etc.
- ◆ There are some occasions when we have to allow others to take control or relinquish our own sense of control for the sake of our mental health and wellbeing. For example:

- ❖ As passengers flying in an aeroplane, on a speeding train or travelling underground on the Tube
- ❖ When seriously ill and in the hands of a surgeon
- ❖ When perfectionism has become frustration and a burden which is leading to isolation, overwork, bad health and stress
- ♦ There are some things, which take place beyond our control. For example:
  - ❖ It is a matter of luck into which society and country you are born
  - ❖ Events, such as natural disasters or man-made atrocities
  - ❖ The unfolding tapestry of life, for the future is largely unknown and while we can to some extent make preparations, for all of us the certainties of life can be turned on their head and change can happen in an instant
  - ❖ We are all mortal and one day will pass from this life

Wherever you position yourself on the external/

internal control continuum, ultimate personal control rests in our mental outlook. We can make the decision how to respond in given circumstances and shape our mental world, so determining our experience.

Here are some examples of prominent individuals who have illustrated personal control in terms of their mental outlook:

- Viktor Frankl
- Nelson Mandela
- Douglas Bader
- Malala Yousafai
- Steven Sutton
- Gill Hicks
- Ernest Shackleton

Self-Awareness Check

Decision Making
Planning
Locus of Control

"You are your choices."

Seneca

Locus of Control

- Where do you position your own locus of control?

- Would it be helpful on occasion to take a different position?

- Consider, are you doing things because you think you should? Are you doing what really matters to you?

- Are you trying too hard to predict the future? Life unfolds bit by bit before us. Therefore, while it can be useful to plan ahead, it is important to focus on the present.

- Remind yourself that you have control for your minute by minute choices and decisions.

Building your Resilience

Mental Control &
Mental Outlook

Cognitive Processes
How we think
Change

"If you want to succeed, you should strike out on new paths, rather than travel the worn paths of accepted success."

John D. Rockefeller

Change & Everyday Resilience

When a change is imposed upon us it disturbs our sense of certainty and in turn can undermine our resilience. We are left off balance, out of kilter and in some circumstances it can feel that the whole world has been tilted on its axis. However, we can use the experience as an opportunity for learning and building resilience.

- ◆ Change:
  - ❖ Can happen in an instant
  - ❖ Can be welcomed
  - ❖ Can be feared
  - ❖ Is uniquely experienced
- ◆ Changes delivered upon you might be:
  - ❖ Bereavement
  - ❖ News of illness
  - ❖ A new job or changes to job conditions
  - ❖ The breakdown of a relationship

- ❖ Alteration to your life due to an accident
- ❖ 'Empty Nest' syndrome

During the 1960's Elisabeth Kubler-Ross developed a model, which related her theory of the emotional stages experienced with respect to death and dying

Out of the model developed by Kubler-Ross, a framework for managing change and transition has been adopted and applied by many practitioners in the field of learning and development, to explain the circumstances surrounding many disparate situations. Shown below, the framework is used in a **very simple example,** which illustrates the step processes experienced when we go through change and the certainties of life are disrupted

Imagine that you suddenly find yourself running late for an important appointment when as you are leaving home you cannot find your keys! Your sense of certainty has been altered:

- It's a **shock** as you thought you knew where the keys were
- Time is getting on – you can't believe this is happening – you are in a **state of denial**.
- Now you're getting **frustrated**. You might even start to get angry or upset as you search high and low
- You give up; you think that you have no chance of getting to your appointment on time now. You become '**depressed' and fatalistic**
- Then again you think that you will try to slow down and take a different approach and so you **experiment** with the idea of retracing your actions when you last had the keys
- You **make a decision** that from now on you are going to put your keys in the same place each time so that this situation does not arise in the future

- Your decision to put the keys in a particular place is **integrated** into your daily life and is successfully implemented

The same stages can as easily be applied to other examples. For instance, a relationship breaks down:

- Even if you know the relationship is drawing to a close it may be a **shock** to your system, your emotions are turned upside down and the pattern of life has been changed
- *'This can't be happening' 'S/he'll be back'.* You are in a state of denial and in your own mind you may try to **minimise the impact.**
- **Frustration** manifests as discouragement or disappointment. Alternatively, you might feel embittered or experience resentment. You may start to bargain *'I can change' 'If I do something different things will be better'.*
- **Fatalism sets in.** You blame yourself. You tell yourself *'It's my fault, I should have*

stopped it from happening, and I'm a failure'. You are soul searching. Your energy might be sapped. You may become **depressed**

♦   As time goes on you start to move forward by taking different steps. You begin to accept the situation and start the process of **letting go.** You begin to re-engage with other people, you might **experiment** with trying out new things like taking up different hobbies

♦   You **make a decision** to move forward. You don't want to let what happened in the past spoil your future

♦   You are ready for a new beginning. You have learned from the experience and **integrated** that **knowledge** into your new life

Change & Everyday Resilience

When certainty is destroyed or broken down:

- It can take moments, days, months or years to go through the stages of change. There are no time limits
  - ❖ Have patience with yourself
  - ❖ Recognise that you are going through the steps as described in the examples shown above
- We can get stuck anywhere along the way; Refusing to believe the evidence before us, getting bogged down in a quagmire of resentment or being ground down by a low mood. For example, the children of separated or divorced parents can hope for years that their parents are reunited and the status quo returned. In some cases, individuals decide that all men/women are not to be trusted based upon the actions of one person and so close off to the possibility of finding a new partner
- Transition means that the end of a situation has taken place, even if you think you are standing still, change will be happening around you and although time itself may not be a healer, time will always bring with it a new state of affairs

- The phrase *'What if...'* does not alter things
- When you are ready consider:
  - ❖ Your options
  - ❖ What would happen if you did X or Y?
  - ❖ The things that you have to do to move forward

If you are dealing with the passing of a loved one:

- Consider how the person would like you to be living your life now. It is unlikely that they would want you to be made unhappy with grief
- Although it is difficult, if the last time you were together was not what you would have planned or you are filled with regret, try to recognise that the sum of your relationship was more than those moments; try to focus on the positive events and times
- Make a conscious decision to start a new phase of your life and to build fresh memories

- Mark the anniversary by making a positive plan of what you are going to do
- Time doesn't heal it merely elapses. Occasionally things will trigger your mind, but remind yourself that you have the power to get back on track

Self-Awareness Check

Change

"When one door of happiness closes, another opens; but often we look so long at the closed door that we do not see the one which has been opened for us."

Helen Keller

Learning from change

Identify a situation/experience of change:

- What happened? How did it happen? Where and when did you experience the situation/change?
- As you went through the experience of change, what did you think and feel?
- What did other people observe or perceive?
- What support did you have?
- What action did you take in response to the situation/change?
- Who or what helped you to deal with the situation/change?
- Who or what hampered the situation/change
- How did you know that things were drawing to a close and that you had come through the situation/period of change?
- What have you learned about change?
- Knowing what you now know, what would you have done differently?

- What would your advice be to others dealing with challenging situations or with a change to their circumstances?
- How can you use your experience of change to help you with future changes?

Alternatively, do you need to acknowledge that you are stuck somewhere in the cycle of change and need support to move forward? Have you:

- Become isolated?
- Felt in a low mood and depressed for some time?
- Lost faith in yourself and in other people?
- Become overwhelmed by guilt or shame?

Remember, that change can be tough, it can take time and you may experience setbacks but if you are realistic and gentle with yourself you will come through to the other side.

Building your Resilience

Understanding interactions with other people

The Foundations of Behaviour

There are many forms of resilience…

Richard Branson

Photograph: Courtesy Helga Esteb / Shutterstock.com

As it's fairly well known that Richard Branson struggled at school and dropped out age 16, he has talked of having dyslexia and how that affected him in early life.

However, Branson has proved time and time again the natural resilience he has.

In his own words he says "I have made hundreds of mistakes. I'm sure I'll make many more this year, and learn valuable lessons from every error."

Source:
Virgin.com – My Greatest Failure

Examples of Resilience

Mental Outlook
Richard Branson set up his first business as a teenager displaying a great sense of self-belief. He has throughout his adult life displayed that he has a strong locus of control. He has made his own 'luck' and influenced and created his own world, which in turn has had an impact across the globe.

Recovery
Despite his obvious success, Richard Branson has also experienced setbacks and business pressure. Nonetheless, rather than withdrawing, he has overcome these events and continued to forge ahead with determination and new ideas.

Learning
Branson's philosophy of life illustrates that daring to try new things may lead to mistakes and failure but that in all these events there is an opportunity to gain new insights and expand awareness. He recognises the value of learning from experience and using his observations to the betterment of himself and for others, in turn fuelling his self-belief and putting him in a position to meet life's difficulties from a position of wisdom and understanding.

What 'makes us tick'

People often refer to the nature/nurture debate to attempt to explain behaviour; the fact that this debate creates such a dilemma demonstrates the complexity of actions. The interactions and behaviour of people is influenced by an interplay between different components. When you are interacting with other people and observing behaviour what you are seeing or hearing is more than what is immediately in front of you. You are being presented with a mixture of the following factors:

- ◆ Biological dimension
- ◆ Mental dimension
- ◆ Social/experiential dimension

The multitude of influences upon a person means that they live and view life from their own unique vantage point. Equally, you will live and view life from atop your own vantage point. The result may be that while each have been exposed to the same events, phenomenon and shared occurrence, experience is always personal and so may be distinct from that of others. There will always be areas of difference to recognise and take into consideration during interactions.

Some examples of <u>Biological factors</u> that underlie and may drive an individual's behaviour:

- Hereditary factors
- State of health/illness
- Imbalance between chemical transmitters:
  Can be born with an imbalance
  An imbalance can occur during illness
- The side effects of prescribed drugs

- The effects of chemical stimulants for example, steroids, alcohol or non-prescribed drugs
- Age – changing abilities
- The 'Selfish Gene' (survival of the fittest & competitiveness)
- Hormonal changes & imbalances (for example levels of Testosterone in both men and women)
- Neurological disorders

Some examples of <u>Mental factors</u> that underlie and may drive an individual's behaviour:

- Level & types of intelligence
    - ❖ Verbal intelligence
    - ❖ Emotional intelligence
    - ❖ Practical Intelligence
    - ❖ Problem solving

- Schemata, scripts, frameworks

- Egocentric – may lack the mental capacity to see how things are for other people
- Constructs of how you see people. For example:
  - ❖ Good/Bad
  - ❖ Threatening/To be pitied
- Personality type. For example:
  - ❖ Thinking/Feeling
  - ❖ Judging/Perceiving
  - ❖ Introverted/Extraverted
- Memory. For example:
  - ❖ Ability to recall
  - ❖ Memories of early events can project unacceptable feelings onto our interpretation of other people

Some examples of <u>Social/Experiential</u> factors that build up layer upon layer to influence an individual's behaviour:

- Upbringing or learned behaviour. For example:

- ❖ Neglect
- ❖ Abuse
- ❖ Cared for, encouraged and nurtured
- ❖ Type of family. For example:

    Quiet families *'We mustn't upset the neighbours'*

    Angry families *'Nobody is going to get the better of us!'*

- ❖ Inherited behaviour – that which runs in families
- ❖ Siblings (even as part of the same family the parenting received and experienced by one child will be different to that received by another)
- ❖ Position in the family
- ♦ Social class
- ♦ Race
- ♦ Religion
- ♦ Sexuality
- ♦ Marital status
- ♦ Media
- ♦ Culture. For example:
    - ❖ Nationality
    - ❖ Region
    - ❖ City or Town

- ❖ Road/Street
- ❖ Community
- ❖ The type of neighbourhood in which you live
- ◆ Identification with a group, team, ideology, belief, fashion, etc.
- ◆ Type of education
- ◆ Experience of education
- ◆ Type of work
- ◆ Experience of work. For example
  - ❖ Position at work
  - ❖ Level of autonomy
- ◆ Travel
- ◆ Life experiences. For example:
  - ❖ May have been a victim of crime
  - ❖ May have experienced conflict and war
- ◆ Generational aspect, characterised as:

  Veteran (b.1939 – 1947)

  Baby Boomer (b.1948 – 1963)

  Generation X (b.1964 – 1978)

  Generation Y (b.1979 – 1991)

  Generation Z (b.1992 – 2008)

Building your Resilience

Understanding interactions with other people

The id, the ego, the super ego

Understanding our interactions with other people.

The adage, no man is an island is quite true when we consider our resilient self. For resilience is underpinned and strengthened through our relations with others. To sustain and enhance our resilience we are helped by the:

- Support of other people
- Cooperation of others
- Friendship of at least one or more people

Therefore, it is helpful to understand the nature of interactions, to adapt ourselves, to be most effective and to provide support, cooperation and friendship to others.

Freud organised the machinery of our minds into three parts. These three elements interrelate and the relationship between the parts is theorised to underpin our wellbeing and our behaviour. Equally, the machinery of our mind can lead to anxiety, defensiveness and the projection of undesirable impulses onto others.

The id

The id is the part of us that represents our primary drives and is characterised as follows:

- Immediate gratification
- Impulsive wishes
- Instinctual passions
- Satisfying the instinct for fulfilling pleasure
- Drives, biological needs such as hunger, sex, thirst
- Has no conception of good or evil
- Has no concept of ethics, codes of conduct or other guiding principles

The super- ego

The super-ego is the part of us that embodies the

influences and demands that have come from or are represented in the world around us and in turn have become part of our own internal world. The super-ego is characterised as embracing:

♦ Influences from the world around us including people who have been significant to us as we have grown beyond original guiding pressures

♦ Guiding messages initially communicated to us during our upbringing. For example:
  ❖ *'You must, you should, you ought'*
  ❖ *'You must not'*
  ❖ *'You need to be punished'*

♦ Messages initially communicated to us which have primarily led us to modify behaviour based on for example the:
  ❖ Fear of losing love
  ❖ Fear of aggression
  ❖ Fear of being humiliated

❖ Desire to try to imitate those that we admire
❖ Desire to try to imitate those people we want to impress
❖ Requirement for approval

♦ The sense that we have not met or been deemed not to have met the demands of the messages initially communicated to us leading to a sense of:
  ❖ Guilt
  ❖ Inferiority
  ❖ Being deserving of our *'just deserts'*

The ego

The ego is the part of us that represents development and learning. It is that part of us that has been modified by the world around us and is driven by memories, constraint and repression, perception and problem solving. The ego develops us beyond our primary forces. The ego may try to shape itself to identify with those influences that it references as ideals. The ego is characterised as follows:

- ◆ Reality
- ◆ Reasoning
- ◆ Compromise
- ◆ Choices about the timing, the gratification or the suppression of those elements composing the id
- ◆ Adapting
- ◆ Choosing whether to act on needs
- ◆ Managing the phenomenon that provides stimulation
- ◆ Pursuing pleasure but not at any cost (as is the case of the id)

The interplay between the id, the ego and the super-ego

- Freud is said to have described the id as being like a horse and the ego as being like the rider.

- It is worth remembering in your interactions with others that when people are behaving in a particular way there is a contest being played out unconsciously, through the pre-conscious or consciously between competing forces. Your own behaviour is equally complex and subject to the conflict between the id, the ego and super-ego.

- When you are engaging with other people, you are interacting with the anxieties, defensive mechanisms and consequences of the id, ego and super-ego. In turn this may create discord if energies are out of sync.

Building your Resilience

Understanding interactions with other people

Transactional Analysis
Parent, Adult, Child
Ego states

Understanding our interactions with other people

- ♦ Freud organised the machinery of our minds and largely explains our intrapersonal behaviour. Over 60 years ago Eric Berne organised the machinery of our social world and largely explained our interpersonal behaviour and in doing this was the originator of Transactional Analysis.
- ♦ Transactional Analysis enables us to examine the structures with respect to the social transactions that take place between individuals.
- ♦ At the heart of the theory of transactional analysis is that individuals display behaviour related to particular states, which are called Ego states. In straightforward terms, the approach and attitude we internally adopt or that we take when interacting with others is likely to be overtly communicated from the standpoint

of the Child Ego state, the Parent Ego state
or the Adult Ego state.

Ego state – The Child

- The Child Ego state is a manifestation of the traces of our childhood thoughts, feelings and behaviour. As we grow older behaviour is modified to be age appropriate but at its core are the precepts of the child within.
- Berne identified different aspects which epitomise the child within all of us termed as the Natural Child (which embraces the Little Professor) and the Adapted Child:

Natural Child

The Natural Child within us is characterised as
follows:

- Spontaneous

- Speaks their mind, without thinking of the consequences
- Is without guile
- Innocent
- Lacks empathy
- Uninhibited
- Loving
- Fun loving
- Demanding
- Self-indulgence
- Self-Centred

Typically, the Natural Child will use words like:

- *'Wish'*
- *'Hope'*
- *'I wonder?'*
- *'Wouldn't it be nice if...?'*

Typically, the Natural Child is likely to display the following types of behaviour:

- Giggling
- Whispering
- Playful

- Whimsical
- Spontaneous
- Joking

Little Professor

The Little Professor is characterised as follows:

- Curious
- Tries things out
- Inquisitive
- Puzzled

Typically, the Little Professor within us will use words like:

- *'Why'*
- *'How'*

Typically, the Little Professor will display the following approach:

- Spontaneity
- Creativity

♦ Thoughtfulness

Adapted Child

The Adapted Child demonstrates behaviour in response to external influences, this usually being the early influence of parents, guardians, the family and social background. The Adapted Child may be characterised on a continuum from loud and angry through to compliant and even docile. The Adapted Child is characterised as follows:

♦ Demanding
♦ Must have
♦ Tantrums
♦ Angry
♦ Manipulative
♦ Vengeful
♦ Quiet
♦ Timid
♦ Seeks approval
♦ Tries to be pleasing

Typically, the Adapted Child will use words like:

- *'I won't'*
- *'I can't'*

Typically, the Adapted Child will display the following behaviours and approach:

- Plays one person off against the other
- Pleading
- Rebellion
- Shouting
- Screaming
- Whining
- Crying
- Sulking
- Whispering
- Sarcastic 'jokes'
- Guilt
- Blaming of others
- Compliance
- Dependency
- Shame
- Inhibition
- Withdrawal

We all have within us a propensity to behave from a childlike position but the behaviours and approach played out in adulthood are likely to be a little subtler and so socially more tolerable and acceptable.

Ego state – The Parent

The Parent Ego state is the thoughts, feelings and behaviour, which adopt and emulate representations of parents/guardians/carers either as embodied as critical and controlling or promoting growth and support from a nurturing standpoint. Therefore, The Parent Ego state is classified into two parts, the Nurturing Parent and the Controlling/Critical Parent.

Nurturing Parent

The characteristics of the Nurturing Parent position are as follows:

- Comforting
- Helping
- Kindly words
- Encouragement
- Gently cautioning
- Teaching
- Giving sympathy
- Demonstrates care

Typically, the Nurturing Parent will use phrases/words like:

- *'Well done'*
- *'Splendid'*

Typically, the Nurturing Parent will display the following behaviours and approach:

- Arms around the shoulder
- Drying tears
- Concerned
- Providing hugs and kisses

Critical Parent

The characteristics of the Critical Parent position are as follows:

- Punishments
- Tough
- Disciplinarian
- Rigid or prohibitive rules
- Pushy
- Strict
- Overpowering
- Over controlling
- Forceful
- Crushing
- Prejudiced
- Correcting
- Admonishments
- Inhibiting
- Authoritarian
- Judgemental

Typically, the Critical Parent will use

phrases/words like:

- *'You'll never amount to anything'*
- *You're hopeless'*
- *'Don't'*
- *'Never'*
- *'Always'*

Typically, the Critical Parent will display the following behaviours and approach:

- Stern
- Critical
- Angry
- A raised eyebrow
- A wagging finger

While we may behave in such a way as emulates the position of a parent/guardian/carer. It can also be the case that we are simultaneously motivated to behave due to the messages we received and absorbed while maturing into fully grown people;

Berne described this phenomenon as a type of programming which he referred to as scripts or drivers.

Hence we may consider we have developed self-determination as functioning adults but still be highly influenced by early messages such as:

- *'Be perfect'*
- *'Be strong'*
- *'Try harder'*
- *'Hurry up'*
- *'Please others'*
- *'You can't trust anyone'*
- *'All men are unreliable'*
- *'Big boys don't cry'*
- *'Don't...'*
- *'You can't rely on anyone'*

Ego state – The Adult

The state referred to as the Adult Ego state is the representation of understanding and comprehension. The Adult Ego is the state of being that recognises and computes authentic evidence and data.

Adult Ego State

When function from the position of the Adult Ego state characteristics are as follows:

- Problem solving
- Learning
- Moderate
- Reasoning
- Accepting
- Considerate
- Thoughtful
- Responsible
- Considers different options, implications, outcomes

Typically, the Adult will use phrases/words like:

- *'I understand'*
- *'Is it practical'*
- *'What's your opinion?'*

Typically, when positioned in the Adult Ego state the following behaviours and approach are likely to be displayed:

- Attentive
- Alert
- Constructive
- Listens
- Thoughtful
- Analytical
- Tactful
- Shares experience
- Shows empathy
- Evaluative

- At a basic level, when interacting with others, each person is likely to be **behaving**

from a position either as a child, a parent or an adult.

♦ **Complimentary transactions** result from exchanges whereby the position from which somebody has made a communication receives a response which is in harmony with the nature of the communication. For example, as from a Parent to a Child, an Adult to an Adult, a Child to a Parent. These types of transactions contribute to our wellbeing and get things done. Hence our resilience is maintained.

♦ Occasionally transactions are out of sync. For example, you may think that you are **talking to someone as an Adult but their response comes from a Child position** and is as addressed as to a parent. This is where people get their 'wires crossed' and is so called a crossed transaction. In terms of resilience, the reaction and response that you get from others may in a sense have nothing to do with you as a functioning individual, rather it is a position, which is energised as the predominant psyche of the other party.

♦ There may be occasions when somebody appears to be engaged in a particular type of communication, but they actually have another agenda in mind. This is called an **ulterior transaction**; things are not as they seem on the surface. For example, the phrase *'Would you like to come in for a coffee'* after a date has become a cliché with an ulterior meaning.

♦ In a corporate, business or day to day setting with people who are not close associates, you will probably be looking to engage in **Adult to Adult** communication.

♦ With people with whom you are close, there may occasionally be times when it is good to have some fun, let go and engage in **Child to Child** behaviour.

♦ Sometimes we all need to feel the comfort, respect or affirmation of others and this is when it is good to give and receive support from the position of the **Nurturing Parent**.

♦ Having an understanding of the transactions that take place when people communicate and why you may yourself adopt particular positions with respect to Ego states is important to resilience because it enhances:

❖ Personal self-awareness

❖ Personal control

❖ Reduces misunderstanding

❖ Helps you to achieve personal autonomy

❖ Enables you to achieve intimacy with others

❖ Gives you a choice in how to behave

Building your Resilience

Understanding interactions with other people

Effective approach and behaviour

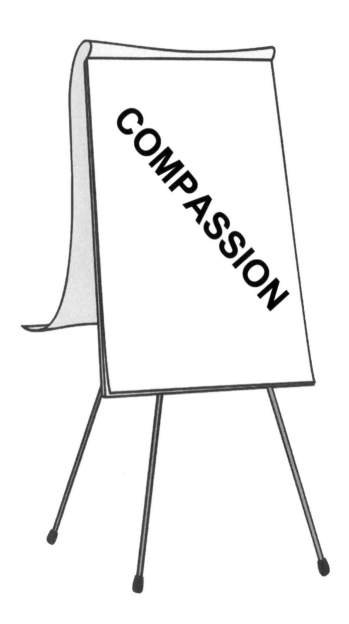

Effective Approach

- Develop understanding of others
- Understand that interaction is driven by many components including the machinery of our minds, as identified by Freud and the manifestation of behaviour resulting from the Ego states, recognised by Berne
- Be tolerant of others
- Ignore hostility and attempts to provoke you. Stay cool
- Show compassion for others
- Have your own values
- Value the views and opinions of others

Effective Behaviour

- Use assertive techniques
- Be attentive and listen
- Find common ground
- Demonstrate understanding and empathy

- Demonstrate behaviours that engender trust
- Participate in mutual problem solving
- Show respect for others
- Be reliable, keep commitments and promises
- Do not belittle or harm others and embarrass or let yourself down
- Engage in ethical behaviour
- Prevent and end harm to others
- Be cooperative in dealings with others

Self-Awareness Check

Interactions with other people

When interacting with others bear in mind that:

- Most people's lives may not actually be as they seem
- The response and behaviour being displayed in relation to you is a manifestation of a complex, interrelationship between internal and external influences, competing states and levels of mental control
- None of us can be in the deep recesses of the minds of others, hence we cannot ultimately predict the behaviour of others

Heighten your awareness:

- Pay attention to what is happening around you
- Put yourself 'in the shoes' of other people
- Consider other perspectives
- Control your immediate impulses. Think carefully before responding
- Consider the consequences of actions

- If necessary, consider changing your own behaviour and so altering the dynamics of the interaction

If you are subject to unpleasantness, hostility, criticism or negativity ask yourself the question, is this justified?

- If there can be some justification:
  - You should behave assertively and choose your response
- If there is no justification:
  - Remind yourself that you may be getting a glimpse of someone's fears, they may be acting from atop a viewpoint relating to their upbringing, behaving with respect to a particular position or driven by different influences
  - You should behave assertively and choose your response

If you are having continuous difficulties with a relationship:

- ◆ Think about the advice you would give to a friend and if appropriate act on that advice
- ◆ Don't try to tackle things alone. Increase your capacity to manage the situation by seeking out help from other people

Employ your understanding of interactions with other people, to improve your relationships and build a network of support

Building your Resilience

Additional ways to enhance your resilience

Mental Control & Mental Outlook

Philosophy of life

- Develop an understanding and flexible approach to events
- Reflect on what is really important to you and reassess your values
- When comparing yourself with others, avoid comparing upwards. The world is becoming increasingly divided, consider the riches of your life
- Release yourself from the rigidity of how life should be:
  - ❖ We all make mistakes
  - ❖ People are fallible
  - ❖ People have shortcomings and limitations
  - ❖ People occasionally break promises
  - ❖ People sometimes forget to say thank you
  - ❖ Planes, trains, buses don't always run to schedule

- ❖ Sometimes life just isn't fair
- ♦ Develop tolerance and patience. For example, it is a fact that:
  - ❖ New learner drivers are slow, slamming your horn will be in vain
  - ❖ Supermarkets have queues
  - ❖ Traffic lights change to red
  - ❖ Level crossings do hold everyone up to let trains pass
- ♦ Think about the meaning you give to situations and events:
  - ❖ What is really happening
  - ❖ What does the situation/event really mean to you?
  - ❖ How important is it?
  - ❖ Why is it important?
  - ❖ Where is this issue on a scale of 1 – 10?
  - ❖ Will this issue be important in six months' time, in one year, in five years' time?
  - ❖ What attitude, approach and behaviour are you going to adopt?
  - ❖ What would a successful outcome look like, feel like, sound like?

- In the workplace we are usually familiar with the idea of planning for the future and so managing risks. Consider doing the same at a personal level:

  ❖ Review your life goals. Set achievable goals and plans that you really want to do

  ❖ When setting your personal goals, diminish anxiety and potential disappointment by setting realistic dates, within a personal goal range. This means that you have a goal date, but also a desirable date for achievement

  ❖ Keep a diary or journal in which you list your intended actions for the day and then enjoy recording your progress.

- On a daily basis record those things that you have been grateful for during the day

- Develop your spirituality, find purpose, values and commitment

- Consider participation in 'Talking Therapies'

- Gain a different perspective on life by reading or watching movies about or by:

- ❖ Notable personalities
- ❖ Great thinkers
- ❖ Historic figures
- ❖ Historic events
- ◆ Develop a growth mind-set. Continually invest in yourself. Expand what you know, what you can do and how you do it

Maintain your sense of self-belief

- ◆ Accept yourself:
  - ❖ Enjoy life rather than believing it necessary to gain the approval of others or please others
  - ❖ In a world demanding perfection, wealth and exaggerated lifestyles recognise unrealistic cultural demands
- ◆ Keep a list all of your skills and achievements. The fact that you are reading this means at the very least you are literate!
- ◆ Remind yourself of your past successes
- ◆ Silence your inner critic. Tune out the negative and limiting scripts and tapes that play in your head. Negativity can empty you of power and inner strength

- Move beyond, let go or diminish the impact upon you of past events:
  - ❖ You cannot undo the past but remember that you can change your present and your future
  - ❖ Do not permit the past to continue to exert power on the present
  - ❖ Use thoughts to objectively reframe past events
  - ❖ Re-focus resentments by first acknowledging your mental distress and feelings
- If you can, forgive.
  - ❖ A note about forgiveness:
    Sometimes a situation is too great or overwhelming to allow forgiveness. Sometimes there is a need to manage your suffering while preventing the harm of the past from contaminating your present. Occasionally past events may be triggered or simply pop into your mind. Use the contents of the handbook to regain personal control and to positively direct your thinking.
- Avoid future resentments:

- ❖ Appreciate that most people are usually so absorbed in their own world that they are unaware of your wants, needs and feelings
- ❖ Recognise that people are not in fact mind readers
- ❖ Make sure that you clearly communicate your wants, needs and feelings
- ◆ Diminish regret:
  - ❖ Write down the lessons learned from experience
  - ❖ Change thinking from '*I wish I had…*' to '*I will…*'
- ◆ Distance yourself from guilt and shame – use your experiences as an episode for learning and growing
- ◆ Whatever you are doing, you are a role model for others, show your:
  - ❖ Positive self
  - ❖ Tolerant self
  - ❖ Nurturing self
  - ❖ Integrity
- ◆ Be determined

"If you think you can do a thing or think you can't do a thing you're right."

Henry Ford

"Our greatest glory is not in never falling, but in rising every time we fall."

Confucious

Self-Maintenance & Recovery

Building your inner strength

- Support and relationships
  - Find someone you can trust completely and talk to them
  - Find someone with a positive outlook you can talk to
  - Accept a helping hand when it is offered
  - Manage your interactions with others:
    Use positive self-talk
    Adopt a calm and happy disposition
    Adopt an assertive approach
  - It is often said that we hurt the ones we love – appreciate and treat with respect the people in your life who really are important
  - Keep close to you photographs or a set of the names of those people who matter

❖ Show kindness to others – this will also make you feel good about yourself

Relaxation

♦ Learn how to appreciate and enjoy life now
♦ Enjoy opportunities for laughter
♦ Give yourself small treats
♦ Engage in absorbing pastimes. Develop hobbies that get you in flow, in other words you become so absorbed you lose track of time. Enjoy being in the 'zone' doing something because you want to do it, not because you have to do it
♦ Enjoy activities and visit places such as:
  ❖ Exhibitions and displays
  ❖ Galleries
  ❖ Libraries
  ❖ Country Parks
  ❖ Countryside
  ❖ The coast
  ❖ Events
  ❖ Concerts
  ❖ Theatre
  ❖ Museums

Recreation time spent such as visiting exhibitions or going to the theatre can help to alter perspective. Being in touch with nature can give you a boost, as it provides an opportunity to enjoy the blessings and abundance of life.

◆ Give yourself something to look forward to by planning days out, weekends and breaks
◆ Absorb yourself in an enjoyable book
◆ Immerse yourself in some music: Choose music that lightens your mood and lifts your spirit
◆ Engross yourself in planning and doing something that you haven't done before such as designing part of a garden, or producing a meal that you haven't cooked before
◆ Create a list of 'Mood Shifters', this is a list of those things that you know when brought to mind will give you a bit of a lift

- Meditate: Use techniques to refresh the mind and/or to find answers to questions
- Control your thoughts:
  - ❖ Recognise triggers and learn to regulate your thoughts and attention
  - ❖ Practice mindfulness. Pay attention to what is going on now. Notice when your thoughts, emotions, problems and anxieties are streaming into your head and taking over. Drown them out for a few minutes by paying attention and connecting to the present moment. Focus on one thing or closely observe something and then concentrate on your thoughts, feelings and sensations

Take care of your physical self

- Engage in regular, sensible exercise (choose something that you enjoy and will continue)
- Break your day up by doing something physical, as moving about can change your mood

- Be mindful of your posture and its effect on your wellbeing and in turn the impression you are creating and your impact on others
- Eat a balanced diet. Don't deny yourself treats but eat in moderation
- Enjoy alcohol but in moderation (and as per guidelines)
- Organise your life in order to get sufficient sleep
- Maintain personal hygiene and appearance
- Give yourself permission to rest and to properly get over illness

Be organised and methodical

- Create boundaries between your home life and work life
- Maximise your time by using time management techniques (this will relieve pressure and mean that you have sufficient time to engage in different ways of maintaining your resilient self)
- Follow the adage *'A stich in time saves nine'*. For example, maintain and look after your:
  - ❖ Home or personal living space

- ❖ Work area/space
- ❖ Tools/Equipment/Effects
- ❖ Vehicle
- ❖ Clothes, shoes, bags/luggage
- ❖ Personal belongings
- ❖ Paperwork and bills

- ♦ 'Just do it' don't leave chores and work to pile up. Keep on top of routine activities such as ironing, cleaning, gardening etc.

- ♦ If faced with a problem begin by first establishing that it is your problem, ask yourself the question *'Whose problem is this?* (It may be that you are prone to taking on things for other people that they could be doing themselves). If it is your problem, take a methodical approach

- ♦ Maximise the use of tools, which mean that you are not putting yourself under pressure by relying on your memory. For example:
  - ❖ Applications that provide reminders for things such as birthdays and events
  - ❖ Keeping a journal or diary of what you have been doing and intend to do
  - ❖ Easing the anxiety of forgetting those ideas that simply pop into your head

       through the day and night by keeping a jotter by the bed, in your handbag etc.

- ❖ Systematically and properly storing documents
- ◆ Try not to be a perfectionist

Time management techniques

- ◆ Self-Management:
  - ❖ Practice being more assertive in order to deal with people who take advantage of your good nature
  - ❖ Learn to say No
  - ❖ Learn to say no to jobs that aren't yours
  - ❖ Learn to delegate
- ◆ Preparation & Planning
  - ❖ Plan the day
  - ❖ Keep a daily list of tasks and rank your tasks for the day or week
  - ❖ Identify tasks that are related, especially those concerning the same people and tackle them together
  - ❖ Use planners to enable you to see the year as a whole

- ❖ Set yourself realistic deadlines (including intermediate deadlines)
- ❖ If you can, always try to finish one job before you go onto the next
- ❖ Ensure you have private 'me time' or working time - Book appointments into your diary for 'meetings with yourself'
- ❖ Plan and organise goals

- ◆ Specific workplace time management techniques
  - ❖ Make more use of standard documents and templates
  - ❖ Tidy your work space
  - ❖ Improve storage and filing systems
  - ❖ Unsubscribe from circulation lists
  - ❖ Be careful about signing up to newsletters and updates
  - ❖ Write and respond to e-mails and telephone calls in blocks
  - ❖ Before telephoning people jot down the points you want to make
  - ❖ Be mindful of wasting other people's time

- ❖ Manage interruptions by quickly establishing why someone is telephoning you or has come to see you
- ❖ If necessary, manage interruptions by suggesting a later meeting which is realistically timed and suits all parties
- ❖ If possible, set aside time during the day when you do not accept interruptions (let colleagues know)
- ❖ If working in an open plan office, arrange time to work at home or find somewhere inaccessible to work quietly and without background noise on those things that require special concentration
- ◆ Time management when managing others
  - ❖ Draw up a Skills Matrix of staff abilities, use as an aid to planning delegation, to filling skills gaps and ensuring seamless service delivery
  - ❖ Invest time in training your staff
  - ❖ Identify the time wasters and manage their performance
  - ❖ Delegate activities

- Familiarise yourself with management methods which may:
  - ❖ Eliminate the need to frequently check up on people
  - ❖ Encourage staff to solve their own problems
- Meetings:
  - ❖ Plan in advance
  - ❖ Set and publicise an agenda
  - ❖ Properly manage the agenda, time items on the agenda and manage contributions

"The bad news is nothing lasts forever. The good news is nothing lasts forever."

Unknown

"The meaning of life is to find your gift. The purpose of life is to give it away."

Pablo Picasso

Recovery & Learning

Carry out a personal 'Health Check'

- Evaluate the burdens you are carrying
- Examine the balance and the investment you are making between each of the different parts of your life. For example:
  - ❖ Time spent with the important people in your life
  - ❖ The level of energy and emotional investment you are giving to your work
  - ❖ Indoor and outdoor pastimes
  - ❖ Investment in relaxation such as short breaks and holidays
  - ❖ Health and fitness
  - ❖ Home life
  - ❖ 'Me time'
- Where do you need to invest your time and energy?
- What do you need to do more or less of?

- Identify those areas of your life that are bringing you down
- Identify those areas of your life that energise and bring you to life
- Set goals to diminish the areas that bring you down and goals to increase those aspects of your life that nourish and sustain you
- Positively imagine how you will feel, look and sound like when your goals have been achieved

Note

We all have occasions when we need assistance and support. You are not alone. An aspect of resilience is being able to reach for a helping hand. Therefore, you should seek medical or professional help if you are experiencing long term signs or symptoms or concerned about any of the issues raised in this handbook.

Good Luck

Have courage

Be proud of who you are

To the Point

About the Author

Jacqueline Mansell is a Chartered Psychologist and business owner who has worked in a career dedicated to learning and development.

During the course of her career Jacqueline has reached many people through her work and interventions, and is now bringing her accumulated knowledge and expertise to a wider audience through her handbooks.

To the Point handbooks have been designed by Jacqueline to provide a compilation of her reference notes and presentation materials, built over the span of many years. The handbooks cover psychological themes accessible and applicable to everyday living.

To the Point

To the Point

To the Point

Printed in Great Britain
by Amazon